TIME AS ALWAYS WAS

TIME AS ALWAYS WAS

Selected Poetry and Spoken Word

PJ

PHOENIX JAMES

TIME AS ALWAYS WAS

Copyright © 2025 Prince-James Harrison.

All rights reserved.

No part of this publication may be reproduced, distributed, or transmitted in any form or by any means, including photocopying, recording, or other electronic or mechanical methods, without the prior written permission of the publisher, except in the case of brief quotations embodied in critical reviews and certain other noncommercial uses permitted by copyright law.

For any questions about usage, please email contact@PhoenixJamesOfficial.com

First Edition: 2025

ISBN: 978-1-0685383-7-7 (Paperback)

Cover Artwork & Design by Phoenix James.
Book Design & Formatting by Phoenix James.

Visit the author's website at www.PhoenixJamesOfficial.com or email him at phoenix@PhoenixJamesOfficial.com

Time journeys on quietly,
unable to endure you.

CONTENTS

ALL WE HAVE 1
ARE YOU THERE YET? 3
COMMUNICATIONS 450 YEARS AGO 5
ENJOY YOUR LIFE DON'T WASTE IT 11
FOREVER 16
GATHER 17
GO 19
ICON 20
IN THE PROCESS 21
IN TIME 24
INAUGURAL CELEBRATION 32
IT'S TIME 35
LAST CHANCE 36
LEGACY LANGUAGE 38
MISSING SUMMER 40
NEVER GOING BACK 42
NOTHING BEFORE IT'S READY 43
ON HAVING BABIES LATER IN LIFE 46
ONE TIME AT RONNIE SCOTT'S 49
PIECES LEFT BEHIND 51
POSSIBLE 56
PUTTING IN THE WORK 57
REMEMBERED 61
SEE DIAMONDS 62
SOLDIER SONG 63
THE EVOLUTION OF MAN & MICROCHIP 69
THE JOY OF SHORT TERM SACRIFICE 78
THE RIGHT VIBRATION 80
THE TIME I TRIED JAMAICAN WEED 87
THE UNAWARE 89
THIS TOO IS POSSIBLE 92
TO THE FIRE 93
TO WHOM IT MAY CONCERN 110
TOO SOON 114
TRAVELLING THOUGHTS 117
VICTORY IS YOURS 119
WHEN THE WRITING STOPS 124
WRITTEN WARNING 125
YOUR AUTHOR 128

ALL WE HAVE

We want it all now
Too often
At the sacrifice
Of the things
That really matter
The things that won't wait
The things we need
Most of all
While we madly pursue
The things that will keep
The opportunities
The endeavours
That we feel
May be slipping
Through our fingers
Losing our grasp
Trying to hold onto things
Things
That change form and fashion
As quickly as we do
The wants we finally receive
Become the things
We no longer desire
We've let go

To chase after new ones
The chances
That always
Come around again
Losing sight
Of the moments that won't
It doesn't all have to be now
Because what's most important
Is that now
Is all we have.

ARE YOU THERE YET?

Are you a treasure
Or just a trophy
Are you a nice to have
Or a necessity

Are you the text message
Or the phone call
Are you making an effort
Or none at all

Are you a date night
Or just a late night
Are you the postcard
Or the plane flight

Are you a roller coaster
Or just a bike ride
Are you a mind blower
Or just a nice time

Are you closer now
Or just between the sheets
Are you making actual love
Or make believe

Do you ever question it
Or just accept it
Do you offer it
Or just expect it

Are you the main course
Or the side dish
Does it empower you
Or just impoverish

Are you doing it
Or just on the to do list
Are you the go for it
Or the I wish

Are you a make it happen
Or a wait and see
Are you a definite
Or a supposed to be.

COMMUNICATIONS 450 YEARS AGO

I believe you just had to walk
And hope that the person was home
That they hadn't gone out
Onto a field somewhere
Doing something with their farmland
Which was like acres
And maybe you rode your horse
Or you walked on foot
Until you found them
It might have taken you four days
To find them
But it didn't matter
Because you knew nothing of smartphones
You knew nothing of computers
You knew nothing of telephones
You knew nothing of writing a letter
And posting it
That might have been on its way maybe
I don't know
But you would have just
Looked for that person
You have no way of contacting them
This is before the postal service
It's before computers

Telephones
Smartphones
What did you do
You just walked around for four days
Until you found them
How did it go down
When you had to find someone
But they could have been anywhere
They were without aeroplanes
So they didn't fly anywhere
So they weren't too far
There were no cars
So they didn't drive anywhere far
They would have been around
But what if they decided to travel
On foot for four days somewhere
And they weren't able to notify you
What would you do
I guess you just wouldn't see them
Or you just kept visiting
Visiting again until they returned
That's crazy
Imagine
What if they emigrated somewhere
Before transport
Before cars and planes and buses

People would just disappear
You'd have gone to where they live
Their little hut or wherever it was
And they would have been gone
From that vicinity
They would've taken their stuff with them
And suddenly be nowhere to be found
How did that work
That's quite fascinating
How did it work
When someone decided
They wanted to move somewhere else
How did they get around
I suppose they traveled less
I reckon they traveled shorter distances
Because they couldn't really cross the ocean
Well, then again, they did do that too
Because obviously they built boats
And made rafts and things
Sailing would have been another thing
That was pretty big then
It's amazing when you think about it
The distances
That they still managed to cover
I think there were more communities
Back then

I think people were more together
They couldn't rely on a mobile phone
To message somebody
So they had to keep people close
Messages had to be shared
And promises kept more
I imagine that they kept together more
They kept in their circles more
Because obviously if they did separate
They would have gotten lost
And no means of contacting each other
No cellphone
Can't get back home and email them
And say sorry I missed you
Even if they didn't have a phone
They would have had email nowadays
They would have had some kind of access
To the person through a computer
Or even to write a letter and post it
With the Queen's head stamped on it
Not even that existed
I guess it was just smoke signals
Or sending out the messenger birds
Carrier pigeons
I wonder how far back that goes
I'd love to take a trip back in time

Just to see
How communications worked
Just a comms exercise
Just to experience
How communications were
In the early hundreds
That'd be interesting
Let's say the sixteen hundreds
Or further back in history perhaps
I'm not too sure
Of all that was happening
In the sixteen hundreds
I couldn't really pinpoint
Where I'd need to land
If I went back in time
In a time machine
I'd probably do a bit of research
Before I went
To see what was going on
At that time in history
And then decide from there
Armed with that information
I think a lot of people of today
Would struggle with the sixteen hundreds
I think even the greatest historian
Would struggle with the facts

And real timeframes of things
I think even Google would struggle
Imagine
Anyone that's at Google now
Was not around
And anything that Google works on
Wasn't around
So where does all the information
Come from
Is it passed down
How far back can you really go
And have accurate facts.

ENJOY YOUR LIFE, DON'T WASTE IT

I was talking to a friend this evening
Which reminded me of some thoughts
I was having this morning
And basically
I was thinking
If you're like forty plus years old now
If you look at how quickly that time went
You realise, it was like a blink of an eye
Like twenty to thirty went quick
Then thirty to forty went even quicker
It's like to say, if you live
You've got roughly another forty years
Older people say
That it goes quicker and quicker
The older you get
So your forty to fifty
Goes even quicker than thirty to forty
And then fifty to sixty goes even quicker
Than forty to fifty, and so on
It's like a blink of an eye
So imagine how quick
The next forty will go
If we are blessed with another forty
It's like we don't have fucking time

To waste, really
We don't have time to waste
Sweating on shit that doesn't really matter
That's just putting it bluntly
We're gone tomorrow
We're gone in a second
Our existence is so minuscule
In the great scheme of things
What a blessing it is
To even have seen this shit
What a blessing it is
To even have existed in the first place
We were the sperm that made it
To even be here now
Having this conversation
Interacting with each other in this way
We are the sperms that fucking made it
And we fucking waste so much time
On trivial shit
And things that don't even matter
Things that are just irrelevant
Things that are not even worth the time
When you look at the special time
That we have here
And what we get to experience
In the time that we have on earth

And how brief it is
It's fucking crazy
How much time we ponder
And waste time worrying
About shit that won't even matter
In a year's time or six months time
Or in a week's time
We just get so caught up
That next forty
For those of you who are forty like me
And plus
We don't have much time
We don't have another forty
To spend our lives worrying
About bullshit and crap
That other people worry about
Seriously
We don't, we just don't
Time wasting, time wasting
Do not waste time, people
Do not waste your life away
Even if you're twenty, thirty
Sixteen or whatever
Know that your time goes so damn quick
It just goes, it goes so quick, man
Enjoy your life

Maximise your life
Make the most of it
And enjoy every moment
Don't worry about stuff
That doesn't even really matter
In the grand scheme of things
When you're on your deathbed
And in those last moments
You think about what you enjoyed
Don't let it be regrets
About time that you wasted
Worrying about trivial shit
Like relationships that didn't work out
And hating people for the rest of your life
Carrying that hate and that grievance
All that stuff
Just out the window
Forget it
Today
Because that's all we have
All we have is today
Do not waste your life
Live your life
Have a good time
Whatever you're doing
I mean, just enjoy your life, man

Just enjoy your life
And maximise the time
That you have here
You don't have it long
I'm not going to be here for that long
You're not going to be here for that long
It goes in a blink of an eye
This is all we have right now
Do not waste it
Enjoy your life.

FOREVER

I am not Icarus
These wings
Do not melt
I don't fall
From the sky
I resurrect
The self
I die
And live
Eternal life
In forever
I shall dwell
Amen.

GATHER

If
My eyes
Should see
The eternal shade
Before I finish
All I have to say
May you each
Add one of my writings
To a page
And read it aloud
Beside my grave
To all and any
Who gather in my name
May you also exchange
Words of your own
About the reasons
Why you came
Bring photos
And notes
Share our jokes
And pains
Recall
One of my quotes
Then recite it

Along with a poem
You wrote
Pause a while
And then smile.

GO

Seconds turn into minutes
Minutes turn into hours
Hours turn into days
Days turn into weeks
Weeks turn into months
Months turn into years
And your best days
Will have passed you by
Like a thief in the night
While you were fast asleep
In your bed
Or flutter away
Like a butterfly
While you were daydreaming
At your desk
Don't waste another second
Of the time
That you have left.

ICON

I hope to be
Remembered
And regarded
As both
A great creator
And a good person
So somewhere
Between
God and Jesus.

IN THE PROCESS

The edit
Just wasn't working
I had to go back in
Take it apart
And start from scratch
At the very beginning
Shot by shot
I had to separate the *necessary* shots
From the, what I call
The *nice to have* shots
A process of elimination
Where many of the *nice to haves*
Would be no more
I extended the length
Of the *necessary* shots
To meet the length
Of the overall narrative
Of the piece
It worked very well
In fact it worked much better
Than my initial vision
Of what the final piece
Would ultimately be
It became a smoother

Tighter
More succinct work
Another one of those
More often than not
Cases where
Less is more
Sometimes it just goes that way
Within the creative process
Things change
From how you originally
Envisioned the final look
Sound or feel
Of the thing you're creating
The piece itself
Always tells you
What it's meant to be
And takes you in that direction
If you're willing to listen
And be guided
By the creative energy
You've tuned into
Which is to be open
At all times while creating
Allowing yourself
To be lead
By the same energy

That brought it all to you
In the first place
It can be considered
A give and take relationship
With your self
And creative energy
A collaborative endeavour
A tuning in
An exchange
A conversation
Between you
As the earth
And the greater
Surrounding universe.

IN TIME

Unfortunately, you're a poet
This is the tragedy
They'll say you're a freak
They won't approve
Of you seeking
To forge yourself a reputation
In the world of literature
They'll seek to burn your desire
Your fiery passion
Douse it like water to a flame
But you must rage
And burn bigger and stronger
And greater
Because you have to
They will learn
And you will find
Your proper place
Your immortality is at stake
In the end
When all the words are said
And all the deeds are done
The only name
They'll have ruined
Is their own

And those that follow them
They won't prevent you
From rising
Among them
Yours is the only name
That shall be remembered
And recalled
Discussed
Revered
Quoted
Mentioned
Studied
Many years from now
All will know your name
Your greatest moments
Captured on a page
From the words you've written
That the world will never forget
You have a purpose on this earth
To be a great writer
You never know
When your moment will come
But you can sense it coming
Just write
Let go
Lose control

Keep your mind on fire
A fire that cannot be put out
Keep writing
Your brain exploding with ideas
Let them ignite your soul
And with that, you write
Become the poem
Write hundreds
And thousands of poems
Right where you are
And wherever you go
Never stop writing
They cannot stop you
Write and write and write
Poem after poem after poem
And keep on going
Don't ever stop
It's important
It matters
Who cares
What they say
Who cares
What they think
They don't know you
They never did
But they will

And all those who come after
You don't need them
To acknowledge you now
Your voice will be heard
Forever
And for them
It doesn't even register
Yet
In time
Those who live long enough
Will all understand
That your poems are powerful
Too powerful
In time
You won't believe the reactions
To your writing
The reverence
The respect
Way above and beyond
The ridicule
And remarks
So write
Make your mark
Write whatever you want to write
Say whatever you want to say
Make whatever you want to make

Your poems
Are works of genius
Works of art
They need to be heard
They need to be seen
And they will
By all people
Get ready
Write
Be ready
To see
And be seen
And to witness
For yourself
The greatness of your creations
Your poems, your words
You won't remain invisible
The world will read your words
Everyone will see you
Everyone will hear you
All will feel you
Become who you already are
The world will know your name
You are not a nobody
Think your words
Speak your words

Write your words
Publish your words
Do not let them die inside you
Die with you
Write
Don't disappear from this earth
Without a word
Write
Write the love
Write the joy
Write the hurt
Write the pain
Just write the words
Just get to work
And let them remember your name
Don't worry, they will find you
You will not be hidden
You'll be famous
A famous poet
World famous
Perhaps even famous overnight
You're famous now
You just don't realise it
Just how much
You're discussed in rooms
You've never been in

But time will show
Fame is yours
You cannot escape your fate
Publicity and immortality await
Many are here today
And will be forgotten tomorrow
But not you
Your journey is a different kind
Your calling is a special one
You have mountains to overcome
Oceans to conquer
And wars to fight
But you must fight them
Alone
And ask for nothing in return
Your glory awaits
That the task has been given to you
And you alone
Is both the gift and the reward
Not the acclaim
Not the praise
Not the applause
In time
We are all forgotten
But not you
You will be one of the greatest

And most amazing
Poets to ever have lived
This is who you are
Right here
And right now
Speak it
Be it
You are blessed
And all that live to see it.

INAUGURAL CELEBRATION

We come
From another place
And another time
A place
Where time
Has no place
We are the voices
Of the future
Present
And past
We are yesterday's
Cosmic spirits
And tomorrow's people
We are words
Sounds
And power
Our words
And sounds
Are energy
And have the power
To create change
We are the writers
Wordsmiths
Lyricists

Poets
Modern-day scribes
Griots
Messengers
Thinkers
Visionaries
Bringers forth
Of prophecy
The foretellers
Of the foretold
Documenters
Of the old
And new world
We have no roots
In any organised religion
But all religion
Has its roots in us
Our purpose
Our names
And their meanings
Have been
And shall be
Etched into
And engraved
On walls
And in the minds

Of our children
And their children
And their children's children
We are before
And shall be after
We are sent
And shall send others
There are many of us
And shall be many more
With many directions
And many aims
But among us
One common cause
Join us
In celebration
And remembrance
Of this
That shall never
Pass away
But live
Forever.

IT'S TIME

You are greater
And far more powerful
Than you realise
Your possibilities
To become
Whatever you desire
In your life
Are endless
And infinite
Your capacity
For the achievement
Of any level
Of success
You can imagine
Is beyond anything
You've ever thought of
It's time
To become
All you can
And are meant to be.

LAST CHANCE

I am writing this
For you
So you may understand
The reason why I'm here
And just the kind of man I am
I have a very important purpose here
And one that I must fulfil
For if I don't
Many will suffer
At the hands of evil
And some will even be killed
There are many of us
Who have been sent here
To carry out this gracious task
If it is not accomplished
Our future generations
Will not come to pass
We've been sent out
On an outreach
To touch Gods people of the earth
To raise them up
From their old ways
Showing them
What life is really worth

Our time now is short
But these duties
Must be carried out
We've been coming here for centuries
But our most crucial time is now
Like soldiers for the battlefield
The wise and appointed
Must be brave
And take their stance
Because time is running out
And there won't be a last chance.

LEGACY LANGUAGE

They ask
Why is he so popular
As if it is hype
As if it is trend
As if twenty years of truth-telling
Heartbreak-healing
And line-breaking lyricism
Could be boxed into a hashtag
No
He is not popular
He's resonant
He is what happens
When pain turns into poetry
When silence
Becomes sound
When independence
Becomes empire
He didn't wait for a label
Didn't beg for a seat
He carved a path
From the pavement
With words
That made the broken breathe

Some artists entertain
He awakens
Some follow trends
He leads truths
He's not just a brand
He's a body of work
A mirror
A movement
You don't scroll past him
You stop
And feel
And that's why
He's known
Not because he wanted fame
But because he gave his name
To something greater
A legacy
A language
A reminder
That we're all still rising.

MISSING SUMMER

Again
One of the things
I've really said
I'm going to do
This summer
Is spend a lot more time
Around nature
I've been getting out
To parks and stuff
Hanging out
It's absolutely amazing
It's the first year
I've said
I'm going to get out more
And spend time in nature
And enjoy the sun
Other than being
Locked away
In some dungeon
In the dark
No windows
Working away
Missing
The whole of summer
And then come out
And it's all winter again
I've done that
For many years
And I said

This year
I'm not
So I've been out more
Than I've been in
This whole time
One day
Twenty-four hours
That's it
Twelve hours of summer
Last year
That's what we had
That's why I missed it
I was probably asleep
In the dark somewhere
Probably slept through it
Just asleep
You know
An afternoon nap
I missed it.

NEVER GOING BACK

Technology has taken over
It's like we value that more
Than we do sitting down
And having a conversation with a person
I went through a phase
I was so against technology
Technology is ruining our lives
The robots are going to kill us
And I still think they're going kill us
But now
I'm definitely more on the other side
Of how much it does for us
How beneficial it is to us
And how much we've gained from it
Some people are longing for the old days
They want the old days to come back
But they're not coming back
It's not going to go back
To rubbing sticks together
And smoke signals on the roof
It's not going back there
We have to kind of embrace
Where things are going
And get with it basically.

NOTHING BEFORE IT'S READY

My day has been good
I'm just here thinking
You can't help everybody
You know that saying
You can lead a horse to water
But you can't make it drink
It's so true
There's only so much advice
You can give someone
It's not about the person
Not being capable
Of being completely stupid
It's just about
The just not being in that space
To receive
What you're giving them yet
I like to look at it as seeds
It's a seed that will later grow
When the soil is ready
The seed isn't going anywhere
Because it has been planted
When the soil is ready
Then it will grow
Then it will sink in

And grow
Into something beautiful hopefully
I just felt a little bit drained
From giving that energy
And it just falling on infertile ground
Infertile soil
It's just the way it goes sometimes
I can't help but give
But sometimes
The soil is not ready basically
So I'm just refilling
So I can give more
It's been a good day
I've been reminded
How important it is to give and refill
And that the soil is not always ready
You're pouring the water out
Putting in the seed
But the soil isn't ready
And nothing
Is going to make that grow
No sunlight
No soil
Not water
Nothing is going to make that grow
Until it's ready to grow

Until something is ready to grow
Nothing is going to happen
That is today's lesson.

ON HAVING BABIES LATER IN LIFE

I think if you can
And it's not going to be a complication
To yourself or to your life
And you can bring life into the world
Healthily and happily
Why not
Whatever your age
A friend of mine
His mother had him at fifty
And he's here alive today
Healthy and strong
And we're friends
He's gone on to get married
And have two children
It's great
If his mother decided not to have him
Because of her age
Then he would not be here
To share his life with someone else
And then to create offspring of his own
It's beautiful
I was at his wedding
It's a beautiful thing
That's my take on it

There are of course other factors
That obviously
Would need to be taken into consideration
But for me personally
I think it's a beautiful thing
There's a lot of things
That may make it not a good idea
People often talk about other people
Or themselves being too old and unable
To run around and play with their children
If they were to have them past a certain age
As a reason why no-one should do it
Which is to be taken into account as well
Because by the time they're twenty
If you were fifty at their birth
You're going to be seventy years old
So I get that way of thinking
But I think it's a beautiful thing
I think it's a great thing
That people are able to do that
To still conceive at a certain age
To have a baby
To bring life into the world
I also like to think
That no child will grow up to say
That they wish

Their old parents
Who gave birth to them or adopted them
Much later in life
Decided not to have me.

ONE TIME AT RONNIE SCOTT'S

There was a band playing
I was actually part of a film set there
They were filming a movie
Diana
The story of Princess Diana
Played by actress Naomi Watts
So I was there for that
We were filming scenes for that movie
That was my one time
Being at Ronnie Scott's
So it wasn't actually
A real performance, as such
But the band were playing
In the background of the scene
It was all for that
The scene took place at Ronnie Scott's
I haven't seen the film
I don't know if Ronnie Scott's
Was actually in the film as Ronnie Scott's
Or if they were just out
At a random live music place
Or whatever
But Yeah, that was my one time
Going to Ronnie Scott's

I would like to go for an actual night
Where it's not for work
Where it's not just set up
As part of a movie set
Like with a real band playing
Not actors performing
Stopping and starting
When the director says 'cut' and 'action'
Though of course
They were real musicians
But you get the point
I haven't actually been for a night there
A proper night
It was all work really
It's somewhere I'd like to go
For an actual real jazz night
That would be cool
I really do like jazz.

PIECES LEFT BEHIND

We gave ourselves
To someone else
To laughter
To arguments
To mornings and nights
That seemed endless
But now stretch behind us
Like a road
That leads nowhere

We remember
The hours
Minutes spent
That were ours
Days blended into each other
Nights we thought
We would never forget
And yet here we are
Only silence
A quiet
It hums with absence
Reminding us
Time is gone
No one will return it

We sift through echoes
Pieces of ourselves
Scattered
In conversations held
In compromises made
In love freely given
Somewhere in the quiet
We touch the jagged edges
Slowly begin the work
Of putting ourselves
Back together
Fitting the pieces
Even when they refuse to align
Repair has no schedule
Time demands patience
Hours once spent elsewhere
Now devoted
To ourselves

We feel the weight
Of lost hours
The weight of time
We now must spend
Piecing together the self
Finding the rhythm of breath
The steadiness of our heart

For a while
We don't want anyone
Don't want to share
Don't want to risk
To give again
Means surrendering time
And we are not sure
We have any to spare

In solitude
We find small luxuries
The quiet sun on skin
The rhythm
Of our footsteps
Space
To speak aloud
Without interruption
We wonder
If we ever needed anyone
Or if it was only
Time we sought
Only our own presence
To recognise
Pieces left behind
Pieces lost
In loving someone else

We remember the hours spent
And the ones
We have to spend still
Reflection stretches endlessly
Through evenings
Dissolving into mornings
We feel bitter and tender
The ache of wasted time
Becomes a teacher
Reminding us
Even in loss
Even in absence
Even in solitude
There is growth
There is patience
There is the slow reclaiming
Of ourselves

We gather fragments
One by one
Noticing subtle edges
Smooth parts
Corners that fit perfectly
We realise
We are stronger for the pieces
Even if they remind us

Of hours we cannot reclaim
Even if they whisper
Of love that could not last
As we sit
In our rooms
In our quiet
In the company of ourselves
We breathe
We forgive
We remember
We learn
Time spent repairing
Is never wasted
Even if slow
Even if long
Even if just
The hours we have left
Learning to love the self
Before anyone else.

POSSIBLE

If I'm honest with you
I feel like
Anything is possible
I base that belief
On things I have learned
And experienced
As well as
My own achievements thus far
They are not the world
But they are a part of mine
Part of what is possible
As humble as they may be
I am content
In knowing
That I've done more
Than I ever hoped
Or thought I could do
I aim higher still
I am blessed to inspire
Whilst also discovering me.

PUTTING IN THE WORK

I'm looking at
The next five years
Not next month
I'm looking at the fact
That if I continue doing
What I'm doing now
Everything
That I could possibly want
Will come to me
I won't have to go looking for it
That's just how it works
It's doing the work
And that's
What I'm focused on right now
I can't just
Put up a few videos
And think
How many subscribers can I get
How much can I get paid
It's just not the way I think
It's going to work out for me
I get it
This whole plane runs on money
People want to make money

People want to do things
And enjoy life
I get that
But it's not where
My income comes from
I'm not depending on it
To get rich
Doing the work counts most
Everything else
Comes after that
Ask me in five years
My eyes are closed right now
My eyes are not even open
My eyes are closed to all of that
Because I just want to do the work
I know if I look up in five years
I'll be probably blown away
By what's happening
Consistency and patience
Is the game
That's the whole game
Now that I've learnt patience
What do I do now but apply it
And then let it all play out
All these people that we talk about
They put work in

Before they were anything
I've just stepped in
I'm a baby
I want to do the work
I want to close my eyes for five years
And put in some seriously hard work
I know that all the things
That people want now
When they've just been
Doing it for five minutes
I will get that
By putting in
A hundred times more work
Because
You're not going to get it
For no work
When they haven't even
Left the gate yet
I get it
People just
Don't want to do the work
They take one look at the work
And they think that's daunting
Who wants to invest time
Into doing something
For five years

Just close their eyes
And get on with it
Who wants to do that
People want to do something
For three months
And expect
To see rewards straightaway
Five years is nothing
It was long to us
When we were kids
Five years was forever
But now we've grown up
In our thirties, forties whatever
We see that five years
Is the click of your fingers
That's why I'm happy
I'm happy to put my head down
And just create and produce more
And not look
For any rewards immediately
I know they will come
And here I mention five years
But could be ten, fifteen or more
I'm a firm believer in
If you build it
They will come.

REMEMBERED

I am one of those
Types of people
Who hopes
That when I finally
Leave this world
For good
That I will be
Remembered
As someone
Who gave back to it
Much more than I took.

SEE DIAMONDS

As one door closes
Another one opens
Rarely are truer words spoken
The universe
Works in accordance
To our most passionate desires
Deepest fears
And strongest inner convictions
Thoughts become things
Guide yourself
In the direction of progress
A diamond in the rough
Becomes a diamond on the cuff
Pressure is preparation
Stay faithful
Stay focused
Keep busy
Keep working
Never give up
Never give in
And never stop shining
Better will come.

SOLDIER SONG

Lately
I've been meditating
And whispering
Walking through Memphis
And Saqqarah
Listening for shooting stars
Leaving footprints
In the Sahara
Discretely
Etching my name
On tombstones
And shrines
Collecting chippings
Of limestone
And old bones
Trying to communicate
With the dead
In attempts
To reclaim my eternity
So that you and I
Will never die
But live forever
Permanently
And eternally

Yes
This
Restless
Never surrender soldier
Whose battle won't be over
Until he passes over
So stop trying to define me
Just get behind me
Send word to others
And tell them that they'll find me
On my knees
In Karnak
Washing my face
In the Sacred Lake
Trying to receive blessings
For my journey back
Back through the crossroads
Been on this planet thirty times
And I've still got to think hard
Which way to go
So don't disturb me
I'm busy
Otherwise engaged
Trying to stay connected
Been mastering phonetics
And channelling spirits

Mixed with neurolinguistics
So that when I spit these lyrics
They stick
Creating road maps
To redirect a troubled soul
And I feel like time is short
So don't waste it
Asking me my goal
I have no point to be reached
No specific plan
Just understand
That for my futures
I've been breathing
Into microphones
Relishing the feeling
Of being home
And I'm not far now
Just got to keep creative
Stay focused
And remain blessed
See
A woman told me
She's been reading my poetry
To her kids at night
And in that light
That's more than enough reason

For me to live this life
Push on through soldier
Keep doing your thing
Whenever I come marching through
That's the song the crowd sing
And I surely will
But at the same time
I wonder if they're aware
Of the prices paid to be here
The sacrifices made
To steer clear of pain
And if my enemies realise
It's a blessing
Whenever they mention my name
As my immortality
Dances on the tips of their tongues
And their brains
I can assure you
What was meant to be here
Will never change
So dissect me
Disbeliever
Separate me and see
You'll just be creating
Another way for me to be free
I'm not walking this road alone

No
Take my life
Or let me go
I'll still be going home
Take all I own
But look into my eyes
And know that it is known
My mirror reflects God
And the footsteps of martyrs
And that my make-up
Was designed to take me up
Whenever the going gets harder
You will forget me not
Standing
On the rocks of the harbour
Arms stretched out
Across the wild ocean
In devotion
My skin
Absorbing the sea spray
Of my ancestors essence
Like magic potion
I receive now
My aura
Weighing heavy
Overbearing

And deep-rooted
Like old oak trees
No need to question
Whether I've been here before
Please
See that these lines
Are more than metaphors
And these minds
With closed doors
Will open
In due course
Singing this same soldier's melody
Coming forth
Holding its energy
Remember me
And send for me
Via the source
Bring me my sword
And my horse
Endlessly
A union
Without divorce
Replenish me.

THE EVOLUTION OF MAN & MICROCHIP

I'm coming from
A certain generation
My parents are coming
From another generation
And my grandparents
Came from another generation
In terms of microchipping
It's like we already have the chip
We already have it
We have a version of it already
And we always have
It's just been an evolution of us
And an evolution
Of what that chip is
I feel like credit cards
Were a form of chip
I feel like cash
Was a form of chip
Evolution
From cash to credit cards
To then Contactless
Is a form of chip
I feel it's all a process of preparation
We were talking

About the London buses
And it not being possible
To board one with cash anymore
You have to have an Oyster card
Call that card a chip
Every card has a chip
I feel that's a stage in the evolution
And preparation for what's to come
This whole cashless society
That we hear about so often
I feel the chip is already here
It's all just preparing us for
Not having to have a physical thing
That you're carrying around
I believe in a time
Where you won't even actually
Have to carry around a credit card
And you won't have to have
A contactless card
For transactions anymore
Not very long ago
You always used to have to
Put your card into a machine
And type in some digits
And now you can actually just tap
Or hover the card over a point

And all the information is there
And you make your transaction
I feel there will come a time
Where you won't even have to do that
With any physical thing
Apart from your own hand
Or your eye
Or your finger tip
I feel it will just be a part of your body
That will be the next stage in the evolution
It will be something that's implanted in you
Where you don't have to carry a phone
You don't have to carry a credit card
Where you don't have to carry anything
That has the credit on it
Or has the ability on it to do what you need
You will be able to do it with your own body
Because you will have that thing
That technology
Or that intelligence
Inside of your body
I do believe a time like that will come
We've seen it with animals being chipped
They're talking about in certain countries
How people are being chipped already
It's not like a thing that's to come

There are people living and existing
With chips inside of them already
Working in this way
I'd say it's only something to come
In terms of a wider usage of it
A much bigger population
Living this way
With microchips implanted
As a normal way of life
I think there will come that time
People now don't want to carry stuff
No-one wants to have to wait on things
They want things now
It's not going to be long before
Carrying a phone will seem antiquated
Out-dated and unnecessary
They'll say
What are you carrying that for
Why are you carrying a cellphone
Why would you want to carry that
When you could be like us
You've got to charge that up
You've got to type in the numbers
That's long, man
When are you going to get your chip
Get your chip

You don't have to do any of that
That's just a waste of time, man
Why have you got a cellphone
Who carries a smartphone nowadays
That's what it's going to be like
That will be the conversation
Why have you got that credit card, man
What are you doing
Walking around with credit cards
Who does that anymore
Wow, get your chip, man
Why are you taking so long
To get your chip
That's what the conversation
Is going to be in the future
I feel it's all already in process
So when I talk about the microchip
Already being here from ages ago
Long before the conversations
Even became popular
It's just an evolution
It's preparation
Because I don't think
Anyone is willingly
Going to have a chip
Put into their hand

So there has to be a preparation
It's all gearing towards an acceptance
So whereas
I spoke about the gran
And the mum
And then the child
Who have grown up without it
You will have the generations
In the future
Their children
The children of the children
Or the grandchildren of the children
Who will be more open to it
Because they've grown up
In a world
Where they don't
Have to have a credit card
Or they don't have to type in a pin
They can tap everything
They can tap it, they can swipe it
They can voice activate it
They're being born into that world
So it's more acceptable to them
They're born into a world where
They can have a contraceptive implant
Implanted into their bodies

And that does everything fine
They don't have to swallow a pill
And there's always going to be issues
Because it's not really normal
It's not really human-like
To have something
Inserted into your body
That's artificial
That's not supposed to be there
You weren't born with it
There's problems with everything
That you implant into your body
There's always going to be issues
Of some kind
Until it works properly
There's always going to be
Teething issues
Side effects with things
That are not supposed to be inside us
The contraceptive implant
For example
A lot of people
Are already walking around with it
But think about it
It's an implant
It's amazing to think about

People are already accepting
Micro implants
So it's not that far-fetched
It may be far-fetched for us
Who are of an older generation
Who grew up seeing the change
But people that are being born into it
It's like nothing
It's all a normal thing
You can get breast implants
You can get your lips done
You can get your bum done
These are all relatively new things
If you look at history
So by the time
Those future generations get here
It'll be normal for them to have a chip
They'll say, *Where's your chip*
Why haven't you got a chip
The people who
Don't have the chip
Will be the ones
Who are looked upon
Like you're some alien
Being told to
Get with the times, man

Why haven you got a chip
They'll be saying
Who doesn't have a chip these days
You're in the stone ages
That's how they'll be talking about you
They'll be talking about you
Like you're in the stone ages
Because you've got an iPhone
That's how the future is going to be
People are going to take a look at you
With your Contactless card or device
As if you're some old person
Like you're stuck in the past
Because you're tapping your card
To pay for your items
Or to make the purchase
They'll say
Who does that anymore
I seriously think
We're going to be
Downloading everything
Into our bodies
As opposed to onto a device
I really do believe
That in the future
Such things will be just normal.

THE JOY OF SHORT TERM SACRIFICE

I'm not doing much
Just taking it easy
I'll be updating some stuff online
And that'll be it, man
I'm just taking it easy
Not doing too much
I'll meet up with a couple friends
For a little bit
Say hello
But I'm not going all out
Tomorrow I'll finish some tasks I had set
So I'm not going to be going too wild you
And I'm cool
Because I'm just trying to finish
So I can be on to the next thing
It's like suffer now
And then have the glory later
It's just putting your head down
Head in the books and focusing
And then later on
You can have all the benefits
Making a few moves
That I can smile about later
I don't believe in

The whole work until you die thing
In some job you don't enjoy
Work
Retire
Sweating like a Hebrew slave
For very little pay you
That's not the kind of hard work
I was talking about
I do believe in sacrifices
And giving up certain things
To achieve your goals
And suffering for a while
To actually enjoy life later
Not too much later of course
But after the hard work
I don't believe in working this job
That you hate
Just to have a lifestyle
To impress people
That you don't even like
It's not about that life for me.

THE RIGHT VIBRATION

Experience has taught me
That when you're dating
You have to find someone
On the same vibrational frequency
What that means is
If you're a person
On a high vibration
And the other person
Is on a lower vibration
What happens is
They will attach themselves to you
Because low always seeks high
They are going find attraction in you
And equally
The majority of high vibrational people
Have the desire to help someone
They are drawn to that need
So you're not always immediately
Going to recognise
At least initially
That their vibration
Is noticeably unequal to
And doesn't match your own
It's important to remain
Conscious of the fact

When your vibration
Doesn't match that persons
And also, that they often
Will disguise themselves
In order to seem as if they do
Experience has taught me well
That you have to date individuals
That reverberate and vibrate
On the same frequency that you do
Because otherwise, what happens is
You'll wake up one day
And suddenly think, hold on a minute
This is not who I am
It's not complimenting my highest purpose
Like, this doesn't feel good for me
I have to get back to me
You'll go your separate ways
And that person
Is going to then
Go and connect with another
Who is more on their frequency
It's more likely to be
Someone that is below
The matching frequency of their own
And then what you need to do
Going forward, is to know this
That others have to match yours
So you can't disclose to people

What it is you want in a partner
You have to let them turn up
Just as they are
Without any prompt from you
Which will allow you
To judge them
Based on just themselves
As they come
Because if you give them
All the templates
And coordinates
Then they'll just show up
And impersonate
The type of person
You said you want
When it's completely not them
So definitely make sure
That you're standing guard
At the door of your frequency
And tell yourself, No
I have to find exactly and organically
Where my frequency is matched
Instead of a person
Who is in need of my frequency
who seeks my high energy
To raise their low vibrational energy up
Because that's the only way it works
Low frequency either comes up to high

Or high has to go down to match low
So which one do you want to do
You need to make the decision
No, I'm standing strong and firm
I know what my boundaries are
I know what my worth is
And I know exactly what I want
These are my requirements
And then you have to go forward
And let that person go off
And match elsewhere
With their low vibrational frequency
Because if you don't
You're going to be dragged down
In a direction that doesn't suit you
And your highest purpose
You'll find yourself caught up
Waking up and saying to yourself
Hold on, this is no longer serving me
And it'll be because
You've done the inner work
If they're not doing that work as well
The necessary inner work to grow
As we're always meant to be growing
And moving and evolving
Then you and that person
Are not going to match
And you're going to notice it

So if you are doing the inner work
Be drawn to a matching
With someone like you
Who is also doing the inside work
On themselves
Who is always in a state of
Self-awareness
And conscious evolution
And elevation
Just make sure
That your eyes are open
And you're doing your homework
And maintaining due diligence
Because we all do it
We all make those mistakes sometimes
Even in our platonic friendships
And within our professional world
Anything where we attach ourselves
To people
To places
And to things
That are no longer serving us
If you're doing the work
Make certain
That you're with someone
Who is equally doing the work
Be reminded of this often
Because we are always

Supposed to be evolving
The work is always incomplete
And will remain so
Until we check out of this place
We continuously supposed to be
Always
Aiming to self-improve
In all aspects of our lives
From the inside out
And the outside in
So make for sure
That you are with someone
Who is vibrationally matched to you
And to your frequency
And if they are not matched
You will start to notice
Different little signs
In that person
These days, we call them 'red flags'
You'll look differently at that person
That's why we often look at our exes
And we're like, damn
What on earth was I thinking
Normally, it's not the way they look
It's often much deeper than that
It's normally their mindset
Choices they've made
Their interests

And then we realise
Oh, that's the reason
Our vibrations
Are on two different frequencies
So go where the energy flows
Without seemingly exhaustive effort
And easily, without friction
Go where you know
You are fulfilling your highest purpose
Otherwise, you're going to look up
To where you know you should be
And you're going to realise
And think to yourself
I've achieved not much
By being in this connection
Instead, I wasted a lot of time.

THE TIME I TRIED JAMAICAN WEED

Once I tried some weed in Barbados
I tried some Jamaican weed
And do you know
I slept for half the day at the beach
I slept so strong
That I woke up
And my shoes were gone
My shoes were gone
And my socks were gone
And I had to walk home bare feet
Some strong Jamaican weed, man
I can't even tell you
I don't even know when it happened
And when it took place
I just know
That I was out for the count
When I woke up
I don't even know where I was
I swear to god, man
I had to walk home bare feet
Like seriously
And I will never forget that
That Jamaican weed is strong, man
It's no joke

Worse when you're not a smoker
And you're trying it like me
I'm not a weed smoker
But I definitely remember
Smoking that weed
I don't think it agreed with me at all
I don't know
If because I don't smoke weed
If I was more of a lightweight
And it affected me in a bigger way
Than it would a normal weed smoker
But I'll tell you what
I don't forget it, man
I don't forget that day.

THE UNAWARE

As all types of strange phenomena
Surround the atmosphere
More wool is pulled over the eyes
Of the unaware
I wonder
Do any care
These days and nights
Are so cold here
I struggle
To walk with no fear
As the wicked eyes stare
I feel it in the air
The end is near
So I prepare
As unbelievers
Make a mockery
Of the revelations I see
They make a mockery
Of what could indeed be
Their own destiny
Staying ignorant
To the possibility
Of these things
Ever coming to be

Only the chosen
Understand the prophecies
As global catastrophes
Elevate towards
Their highest degrees
Spreading like disease
And multiplying like flees
Some say times
Can't get worse than these
But we're living in the wicked city
The dark city
Wide, wide world with no pity
It's far from pretty
It's the final times
These could be my final lines
My final chance
To give sight back to the blind
And awaken the sleeping mind
There's still a long way to climb
I'm flirtatious with the rhyme
Because I see the signs
Some things are not right
Everything is not as it appears
The truth has been hidden
And has been so for years
By those

Who seek no less
Than absolute rule
What will become of the people
If they allow themselves
To be fooled
The unaware.

THIS TOO IS POSSIBLE

It is quite possible
That some day in the future
A group of people
Are going stumble
Across someone
Who is doing exactly
What you've done
And are doing now
And will all tell the world
How amazing
And unique that person is
And what a genius they are
And that there has never
Ever been
Anybody quite like them.

TO THE FIRE

Wake up, Supernova
Rise and grind
If you want to shine
Then you've got to put in the time
If you haven't got to go to work
Then why get up at three
Because I love progress
More than I like sleep
Oh that's just way too early
I couldn't do that myself
Well then you just might
Spend the rest of your life
Working for someone else
I'm chasing my dreams
While I'm awake
I'll only miss
The opportunities I didn't take
I'll only lose
If my eyes ain't on the prize
Sacrifice is to choose paying a price
If only five percent are willing to give
Then only five percent will get
The other ninety-five
Will just have to accept whatever's left

Whatever's left is the result
Of anything other than my best
Do better to get better
Expect nothing less
Today
I seize the beast by the horns
My painted face to the storm
Naked as the day I was born
Deep in the thorns
Redeeming all the pieces of me
That were torn
This is the healing
Feeling like I'm reformed
I sit
Motionless
Beside you
And at times
As if outside of myself
Looking down
I watch you
Sleeping
Unknowing
Incoherent
Unconscious
I wonder
About everything it might take

To fully restore you back to life
Even greater than before
I see you now
And know that
All the treasure in the world
Can't compare
To that which is truly alive
You
You deserve more
We fantasised
About winning the lottery
And with the money
All the things we'd do
It's funny I didn't realise
I'd already landed the jackpot
The very day that I won you
There isn't another soul
That I can blame
I threw our winning ticket
To the fire
Watched it go up in flames
You've probably
Burned everything I have
Like I burned everything we had
I'm so ashamed
You fell in love with who I was

Then I pretended
To be someone else
You didn't fall for it
Thank god
I was only fooling myself
A false alarm only I can hear
Inside of a me
Only you can see
A gold spoon
In an empty room
A precious flower
Blossomed too soon
I pray you never know
What that feels like
A stifled scream
In the dead of night
To the fire now
Burn bright
Don't close your eyes
You'll miss the lights
Did a few things
That I shouldn't have done
But done a lot more
That I'm glad I did
What you're aiming for is hard to hit
If you don't know what the target is

And the hardest bit
Is learning
That you were easy work
Yet I so easily
And naively
Made it hard
For us to work
For what it's worth
With
Or without you
It hurts
I feel so deeply entangled
Within my thoughts right now
I can barely piece together words
Tell me
How to craft a worthy
Patchwork remedy
For a broken melody
I'll cast my lot here
And plant a soapbox at your feet
Everyday
Until it sparks a memory
Finally
Speaking without interruption
And now without any idea
Of what more I can say

If I ever told people
I've been coming here to visit you
They'd probably try to put me away
Throw me in some kind of
Mental institute
Some asylum somewhere
For people supposedly
Outside of their minds
Lock us both up
And melt down the key
All just because
They'd never ever find
Among all their precious boxes
One to fit us in
You know
They say
It's not at all about what you know
But what we know
Is it's not who you know
It's who you know who actually gives a shit
Nobody in the world
Cares about your
Grand schemes
And dreams
But you
Yourself

And you
That's it
That's at least until
You can make
Those dreams come true
So make it happen
Take action
Because there's satisfaction
In even a fraction that you do
Show and prove
Paint your city
Make it pretty
And capture the views
Spectacular views
See everything to gain
With absolutely nothing to lose
But the blues
And if you actually do
You'll see this
To be factually true
Alteration in your navigation
Makes your map improve
If you don't like
Where your life is at
Then that's for you
The right solution

To your life's improvement
Lies in wise decisions
And their execution
Let's keep it moving
Little by little makes a lot
It's all about progression
Give it everything you've got
Who laughs doesn't matter
And who matters doesn't laugh
Your task
Is to double up
On what you're doing
Versus how much you care
All you do is keep going
They wont be laughing
When you're there
Architect of your own destiny
Your own future by design
Naysayers keep checking in
Tell them you haven't got the time
And if people
Expect to offer you less
Than you're giving
Then they should expect
That you decline
That's fine

Know your worth
And that the best things
Come to those who work
Earn and live
Live and earn
But nothing comes close
To the gifts you can give
From the things you've learned
Your bridges they can burn
And your tides can turn
But never giving up
Is your only concern
Those who give up on you
Can't expect to get down with you
When you get up
And in this
You can trust for sure
Support is everything
But loyalty
And respect is more
Never forget
What you got in for
For keeps
So dig yourself deep
And explore
Until you find the missing piece

Remember
All things are possible
And nothing is beyond reach
You've heard this all before
I've been saying it in your sleep
And I know you've been listening
Because above the noise
And the toil
I can still hear your heart beat
And inside
I can still feel it
Like it's a part of me
Coming alive
Breathing renewed life
And bleeding new light
Into my existence
Who am I
But a guy
Standing by
Just to witness its brilliance
You could ask me why
But to see you shine
Has been my only mission
And in this instance
I just need you to hide your disguise
Put all your fears and pride aside

And listen
Let your will be strong
Make your will
Stronger than your won't
You won't go wrong
You will succeed where others don't
Believe in yourself
And your abilities
And what you can achieve
And if you can't see your greatness
Or your potential
Believe in someone who sees
Sees it in you
Someone who wont be leaving
Until you see it too
And you profess that it's true
That you're the perfect catalyst
To manifest every gift
You've been blessed with
You
Yes
You've already been
At your deepest darkest depths
That's nothing new
Embark towards
Your highest

Brightest heights yet
You already know what to do
Let your mind be free
Explore each
And every possibility
There's so much more to see
Be who you're supposed to be
You can be down to earth
Or be up to space
Know that your worth
Is much more
Than the world dictates
Feet firmly on the ground
On route to Mars
Your time is now
Be who you are
At one among the stars
A new point of view
You see what you feel
New practices
New politics
New playing field
Stretch yourself
Play for real
Invest in yourself
Make a deal

But of course
I'm a modern day renaissance man
Born in London in the late seventies
What do I know
I know
That if you put your mind to anything
Over time it grows
And so
I'm seeing live with my own eyes
Mere dreams
Turning into real life
I'm encountering souls
Overcoming their own status quos
I'm witnessing
The attainment of goals
I'm seeing doors open wide
That used to stay closed
I'm hearing Yes expressed
Where I used to hear No's
Get up
I've heard too much
And I've seen too much
And I know too much
To just let you go
I can't
And I won't

I'm sorry
But I love you
A gold spoon
In an empty room
A precious flower
Blossomed too soon
I pray you never know
What that feels like
A stifled scream
In the dead of night
To the fire now
Burn bright
Don't close your eyes
You'll miss the lights
Molotov cocktails
In flight
Look like baby fireflies
At this height
What on earth
Could ever be wrong
When after all is said and done
And all have sang and gone
All that will be left
Is this love song to ponder on
All of this high frequency rhetoric
All this poetry

Yes it's poetic
But it's more phonetic energy
Helping me
Set free
All of what I'll never need
Permanently
Forgetting more
Of what I've learned to be
While other mad men
Would walk towards
The edge of eternity
Just to capture
Only a glimpse of you
In the tail end
Of a moon beam
I wake to discover you
Here with me
And absolutely
No part of a dream
You're the heart of me
And the most beautiful thing
In this universe
I've ever seen
You are awesomeness
Incredibly
And wonderfully made

And not by mistake
You are greatness
Personified on the planet
Why are you waiting to be great
Find a way
Or one way make
From there keep straight
And for greatness sake
Try not to arrive late
By your own thoughts
And by your own actions
You'll determine your fate
Throughout all of existence
That which doesn't create
Disintegrates
We've been given rise
Over every tall tree
And over every high place
So it makes no sense to me
Who would ever decide
To only grow halfway
That's only my take though
What do you say
Like who remembers
The embers anyway
What of the smouldering remains

After the glowing beauty
Of the flames
It all melts down
Burns out
Change is the only thing
That stays the same
Ashes to ashes
To the death
Of everything before
Toast to the old ways
Yesterday
A far away spark in the dark
Today a blaze
Wake up, Supernova
Welcome the new day.

TO WHOM IT MAY CONCERN

You knew you were wrong
But still you persisted
Your conscience pricked you
But still you resisted
On and on
You pursued that
Which you knew
Would bring harm
Inside your heart raced
But outside you played calm
For if they saw
For a second
The truth
That was hidden in you
Counteracted
Would be all
That you were trying to do
You sought so many ways
To justify your actions
But to no avail
And to no satisfaction
I heard a man say once
That such people will burn
This is of course

To whom it may concern

Since you willed
Such things to happen
Without raising a hand
Towards prevention
It is fair then to say
The outcome of such things
Has been your intention
And that if there should be
A day and a place
Where all good people
Are mentioned
You shall not be among them
Or be brought
To their attention
It's intense
In the way
That you have neglected
Your inner voices
Urging you
To change your focus
And make different choices
As far as you're concerned
Your agenda is set
And you've made up your mind

Many will forgive
But none will forget
And indeed there will come a time
The days of your name
Shall be blown away
Like the feathers of a fern
This is of course
To whom it may concern

Your decisions
Have caused
Much suffering
And pain
You even hurt yourself
As well as those around you
Under the strain
You cared not
What knowledgeable people said
Would be for the best
You carried on
Inconsiderate
And indifferent nevertheless
It's important to see the karma here
In order to make a change
Or grow
You will only reap

What you have sown here
And this the farmer does know
Realise
That all the good you do
Will be recorded
Against your name
And that likewise
All the bad you do
Will be recorded just the same
For it is through the consequences
Of his actions
That each soul shall learn
And of course
This is
To whom it may concern.

TOO SOON

Post-war
Brutalist
Architecture housing
19th floor
Up above
Everything surrounding
Lift smells like piss
When it's operational
Asbestos walls
Cockroaches in the hall
Shitty pigeons decorate the balcony
Inner city living ain't great
That's just a fallacy
I heard a kid killed another kid
Over a cigarette
Went to prison
And not a word told in the Gazette
One summer time
A big television station
Came and filmed us all
Living in degradation
Just to play it all on our TVs
For entertainment
Old metal electric meter

Only took 50 pence pieces
To keep the power on
That's all the household needed
Lived just a stone throw away
From the primary school gate
Couldn't wait to go home
And play all my favourite tapes
Rode around the estate
On bicycle cruises
Became a champion
Of scrapes
And skateboard bruises
Along with
All of the other young winners
And sore losers
Ball games against the wall
And new friends
Who then only knew
Barbie dolls
And action men
Wild girls
And naughty boys
Grew up fast
And sought other toys
Newsagents
Located just at the bottom of the road

Sold Space Raiders
Stickers
Penny sweets
And Beanos
Who knew
Just what life would've been
When copies of Just Seventeen
Was my favourite magazine
I liked the pop stars and the pop charts
Song lyrics
And pin-up posters
I'd pin up in my room
Before long
It was all over
And we grew up too soon.

TRAVELLING THOUGHTS

What made me get to the point
Of not wanting to hold back on myself
And just being free and letting go
Travelling
Travelling did that for me
Travelling to all the countries
I travelled to recently
And having that space
To be inside my own head
Without distractions
Being away from the familiar things
Being away from my usual routine
We all have our own routine
Being away from all of that
And being able to process
Where I was
Sometimes when you're in something
You can't actually process where you are
And what's going on
Until you're outside of it
So being outside of it
Gave me the opportunity
To look at where I was
And where I wanted to go

Whether I was I happy there
Just travelling
Travelling did that
It just gave me a chance
To open up my mind
And just look out
Being on planes
Looking out the window
Just being able to think
And be in a space
Where I could collect my thoughts.

VICTORY IS YOURS

Take your positions, men
You are the new platoon now
You will take up the banner
Of those gone before
You will be the upholders
Of our divisional territory
You will fight
For first place on the outfield
Don't run from it
Embrace it
It's yours
What are you running for
It's only when you stop running
From your responsibility
As soldiers
In this more so mental war
Than anything else
And stand up and fight for it
Because you owe it to yourself
That you're going to see any benefits
That you're going to see any changes
Because it won't be handed to you
Oh no
That's for sure

It's only when you learn
To control your circumstances
And not have them control you
It's only when you can think
95% solution
And 5% problem
It's only when you do these things
It's only when you can stand guard
At the door of your mind
It's only then
That you're going to reap the rewards
Of true warriors
Fighting without relent
To obtain their God given birthright
It's a struggle
Believe it's a struggle
It's a hell of a struggle
But let me tell you
No battalion
Ever wins a battle butter smooth
Oh no
It's going to be rough
It's got to be rough
Oh yeah
Because it's only through the harshness
Of the experience

That you're going to realise
That the very thing
You fought for
Down in the valley
Is what you're going to celebrate
On the mountain top
If you stick it out
It's only through the harshness
Of the experience
That you're going to be able to
Have a true appreciation
And understanding
Of what the victory means
And why
You fought so hard to get it
If you stick it out
That's why
That's why you've got to face it full on
Not run
Because when you stop running
You realise
You're still unfulfilled
Still incomplete
Still lost
Still searching
And then it hits you

All at once
There's a reason
Why you needed to fight
There's something you wanted
There's a goal
You were trying to achieve
You've run away
And now you're further away
From winning
And overcoming
And obtaining that goal
Than when you started
You're in a circle
And it's only when
You decide to make an attempt
To break out of that circle
Meaning
Stand up and fight
And stop running
It's only then
That you're going to see results
It's only then
That triumph will be yours
It's only then
That you break out
Of that attempting and failing

Attempting and failing
Repetitive circle
That's cordoned you off in the past
From achieving what you really want
It's only then
That you're going to feel complete
It's only then
You're going to feel fulfilled
The outcome of this conflict
Is in your hands
So take your positions, men
You are the new platoon now
You will take up the banner
Of those gone before
You will be the upholders
Of our divisional territory
You will fight
For first place on the outfield
Don't run from it
Embrace it
Because it's yours.

WHEN THE WRITING STOPS

When the writing stops
They say they have writer's block
But writer's block doesn't exist
Writer's block never did
Resurrecting an old myth
A thing that never lived
This scapegoat for their sin
That the gods find no pleasure in

When the writing stops
They think it is writer's block
But those who can write, write
And know that it is not

When the writing stops
You proclaim it's writer's block
While the writers carry on
And when we pause to ask where
Is your illusive muse now
You still tell us of a unicorn
Kidnapped
And held in bondage
By a ghost
That cannot write.

WRITTEN WARNING

If you
Should be so fated
To fall in love
With a writer
Be sure it is love
And love them truly
It is a burden to bear
To love
Such an individual as this
But love them
Wholeheartedly
Love them fully
Love them
Unashamedly
And deeply
Withdraw and flee
From their presence
Immediately
If it is not so
Or if it is not in you
To love them
Freely
And completely
For the mighty sword

They are fated to wield
Gives birth
To both life and death
Thus
Do not deceive them
Do not lie
Do not love them falsely
Conditionally
Or uncertainly
For if they decide
You have intentionally
Mislead
Mistreated
Or wronged them
They will immortalise you
In all the places
Where words are found
Or in one place
Where you'll burn
Forever
Where you will live long
But painfully
And die slowly
And miserably
You will be eternally
Reincarnated

In a poem
On a wall
On a page
In a book
In a film
In a song
On a stage
Out of a mouth
Into an ear
You will scream
Inside yourself
Suffering silently
At the sight
Of your own resemblance
You'll be rewritten
And replayed
Reborn
Then reborn again
Only to live
Forevermore
Spending rereads
And reruns
Of those
Miserable lifetimes
Wishing
You could just die.

THE AUTHOR

Phoenix James is an award winning Writer, Poet, Author and Spoken Word Recording Artist. He began performing his poetic words live on stages across the UK in 1998. His debut spoken word poetry album, The A.R.T.I.S.T, was released in 2000. His first limited edition printed collection of poetry, To Whom It May Concern, was published in 2003. He has toured and performed his poetry internationally since 2004. He has appeared in films, on television and radio shows, and collaborated with other artists, singer-songwriters, actors, musicians, filmmakers and producers. In 2013, he wrote, directed and produced the feature length mock documentary film, Love Freely but Pay for Sex. Phoenix James is the author of numerous poetry books and has recorded and released several spoken word poetry albums including Phenzwaan Now & Forever, A Patchwork Remedy for A Broken Melody, FREE, Haven for the Tormented, With All That Said, Light Beams from the Void, The Love So Far, and over seventy spoken word poetry singles. All are available online now and streaming everywhere worldwide.

If you enjoyed reading this book, please leave a review or comment online. The author reads every review and they help new readers discover and experience his amazing work.

PHOENIX JAMES

Photo by Phoenix James

Phoenix James lives in London, England.

Connect with Phoenix James online via his social media platforms and let others know that you've been fortunate to discover this book.
To contact or learn more about Phoenix James and his creative journey or to receive updates via his Newsletter Mailing List, visit his official website at www.PhoenixJamesOfficial.com

CHECK OUT THE AUTHOR'S OTHER
BOOK TITLES ALSO AVAILABLE
IN PAPERBACK & EBOOK

PHOENIX JAMES POETRY &
SPOKEN WORD COLLECTIONS:

LOVE, SEX, ROMANCE & OTHER BAD THINGS

ROUTE TO DESTRUCTION

DELIRIUM OF THE WISE

DON'T LET THE DAFFODILS FOOL YOU

CALL ME WHEN YOU'RE FREE

FAR FROM THE OUTSIDE

THE ONES WE DIDN'T KILL

LESSONS FROM EVERYWHERE

ANOTHER ONE FOR BURNING

A LONG BRIGHT COLD DARK SUMMER

SHAME POINT ZERO

THE SANDBAG THEORY

SOFT, SEXY & WET

BELOW BASE LEVEL

TO CATCH A PASSING UFO

NOW WE'RE TRULY BEAUTIFUL

WE ALL SHOULD BE AMAZED

DISCOVER THESE AND MUCH MORE AT
PHOENIXJAMESOFFICIAL.COM

Phoenix James Official

www.ingramcontent.com/pod-product-compliance
Lightning Source LLC
Chambersburg PA
CBHW020334170426
43200CB00006B/377